Attachment

Julia Cranney

methuen | drama

LONDON · NEW YORK · OXFORD · NEW DELHI · SYDNEY

METHUEN DRAMA

Bloomsbury Publishing Plc, 50 Bedford Square, London, WC1B 3DP, UK
Bloomsbury Publishing Inc, 1359 Broadway, New York, NY 10018, USA
Bloomsbury Publishing Ireland, 29 Earlsfort Terrace, Dublin 2,
D02 AY28, Ireland

BLOOMSBURY, METHUEN DRAMA and the Methuen
Drama logo are trademarks of Bloomsbury Publishing Plc.

First published in Great Britain 2026

A catalogue record for this book is available from the British Library.

A catalog record for this book is available from the Library of Congress.

ISBN: PB: 978-1-3506-5906-3
ePDF: 978-1-3506-5907-0
eBook: 978-1-3506-5908-7

Series: Modern Plays

Typeset by Mark Heslington Ltd, Scarborough, North Yorkshire
Printed and bound in Great Britain

For product safety related questions contact
productsafety@bloomsbury.com.

To find out more about our authors and books visit
www.bloomsbury.com and sign up for our newsletters.

Liverpool Everyman & Playhouse theatres
present the world premiere of

ATTACHMENT

BY JULIA CRANNEY

First performed on 4 June 2026
at the Everyman theatre, Liverpool

With thanks to Toby Parsons Productions who originally commissioned Attachment

CAST

Paislie Reid Mat

With the voices of
Debbie Brannan
Julia Cranney
Nina Cranosz
Elliott Kingsley

COMPANY

Writer **Julia Cranney**
Director **Kate Treadell**
Set & Costume Designer **Ellie Light**
Lighting Designer **Kieran Sing**
Sound Designer **Noel Jones**
YEP Trainee Assistant Director **Ella-Mei Burns**
Dramaturg **Tommo Fowler**

Production Manager **Jordan Barnes**
Company Manager **Sarah Lewis**
Stage Manager **Snowzie Rose**
Deputy Stage Manager **Laura Thomas**
Assistant Stage Manager **Tilly Forster**
LX Programmer **James Harrison**
Senior Sound Technician **Ian Davies**
Costume Supervisor & Maintenance **Cate Mackie**
Audio Described performance **Anne Hornsby for Mind's Eye**
Captioned performance **Stevie Burrows**
Producer **Sam Longville**

PAISLIE REID | MAT

Paislie started her career as a lead actor in two seasons of CITV series *The New Worst Witch*. Since this early television debut, Paislie has continued to have a flourishing acting career. As well as acting Paislie is associate director at 20 Stories High, the co-founder and artistic director of The

Black Actors Collective and volunteers at Positive Impact facilitating singing, dancing, drama and personal development workshops in her local community. Her mission is to empower, inspire and create more opportunities for marginalised people.

Liverpool Everyman & Playhouse credits include: *Alice in Wonderland* (Liverpool Playhouse) and *Red Riding Hood* (Liverpool Everyman).

Theatre credits include: Royal Shakespeare Company; Frantic Assembly; Open Clasp; Grosvenor Park Open Air Theatre/Storyhouse; Live Theatre; Contact Theatre and 20 Stories High.

TV credits include: *Special Measures* (Channel 5); *Unforgivable, Casualty, The Responder 2, Domino Day* and *Sugar* (BBC); *Brassic 4* (Sky); *Emmerdale* (ITV) and *Tin Star 3* (Sky Atlantic).

JULIA CRANNEY | WRITER

Julia is an award-winning playwright, screenwriter and actor born and based in Liverpool. She is a member of BAFTA Connect and former coordinator of the Soho Theatre writers' alumni group. State-educated and neurodiverse, she originally trained as a writer with the Everyman's Young Writers Programme. Alongside her creative work, Julia is a writer educator with the creative arts education charity First Story, an Independent Visitor with NYAS and a volunteer counsellor with Childline. She is also mum to Nin.

Theatre credits include: the Offie-nominated *Moments* (Hope Theatre, Islington) and *Empty Beds* (winner of the Scottish Daily Mail Award and an inaugural Eddies award, premiered at Underbelly Edinburgh before transferring to the Arcola as part of their EH to E8 'Pick of the Fringe' festival).

Screenwork credits include: an animated adaptation of *A Midsummer Night's Dream* for BBC Teach, three original romcom features for Reel One in Canada (released internationally on Paramount Plus) and she was nominated for the Edinburgh TV Festival New Voice Awards for her debut script of *EastEnders*. Julia co-wrote and co-directed the short film *Measure* with filmmaker Helen Simmons which screened at BAFTA and Academy Award qualifying festivals internationally, winning the Méliès Award for Best European Short Film at the Molins de Rei Film Festival. She currently has a new short, feature and several TV projects in development.

KATE TREADELL | DIRECTOR

Kate is a theatre director from Liverpool. She graduated from the University of Exeter and completed a Masters in Performance Making at Goldsmiths College. After graduating from Goldsmiths, Kate formed the company The Honest Crowd and had residencies in both the Basement in Brighton and at Battersea Arts Centre. After returning home to Liverpool Kate became a YEP Young Director at the Liverpool Everyman & Playhouse.

Liverpool Everyman & Playhouse credits include: as director: *Blink* (YEP Directors' Festival, Liverpool Everyman); as assistant director: *The Story Giant* (Liverpool Everyman); as co-director: *How to Disappear Completely* *and Never Be Found* (Liverpool Playhouse Studio) and *Road* for YEP (Liverpool Everyman).

Director credits include: *Monday...* (On The Verge, Hope St, Liverpool); *Karaoke Tales* (The Rose Theatre at Edge Hill Arts Centre); *Moments and Empty Beds* (The Hope Theatre, London); *Mum Can You Lend Me £20* (tour UK prisons) and *RISE UP* (Paperwork Theatre).

Co-director credits include: *Until They kick Us Out* (For/With/By Festival).

Associate director credits include: *Deep Blue* (Paperwork Theatre).

Assistant director credits include: *Cinderella* (Shakespeare North Playhouse).

ELLIE LIGHT | SET & COSTUME DESIGNER

Ellie is a designer and maker for theatre and the arts. She trained at LIPA and is based in Liverpool.

Liverpool Everyman & Playhouse credits include: *The Lieutenant of Inishmore, Top Girls, Cherry Jezebel* (Liverpool Everyman) and *Dogs* (New Step Theatre/Playhouse).

Other credits include: *Scouse Christmas Carol, Speedo Mick: The Musical, Scouse Red Riding Hood* and *Haunted Scouse* (Liverpool's Royal Court); *8 Hours There and Back* (All Things Considered); *Silverwood* (RNCM); *Light Falls* (Grosvenor East Theatre, MMU); *Beyond Caring* (Durham Gala Theatre); *Of All the Beautiful Things in the World* (HOME Manchester) and *A Very Odd Birthday Party* (Hawkseed Theatre/UK tour).

KIERAN SING | LIGHTING DESIGNER

Kieran is a Liverpool based lighting designer.

Kieran spent three years as Young People and Community Technical Manager at Liverpool Everyman & Playhouse, teaching introduction to lighting, sound, stage and stage management in theatre to under twenty-fives.

Recent theatre credits include: *I Am Steven Gerrard* (Hope Street Theatre) and *Two* (Shakespeare North Playhouse).

NOEL JONES | SOUND DESIGNER

Noel is a digital artist and creative technologist with over three decades' experience working across immersive performance, sound design and real-time systems. Rooted in a fine art background, his practice has evolved through video and installation into collaborative work with choreographers and performers, specialising in responsive immersive environments. His work centres on improvisational technological systems, informed by production experience in touring theatre and installation, and continues to explore the creative potential of new technologies.

ELLA-MEI BURNS | YEP TRAINEE ASSISTANT DIRECTOR

Ella-Mei is a Welsh director and performer, currently part of the Young Everyman Playhouse (YEP) Directors' Programme. She recently took part in Frantic Assembly's Ignition 2025 programme and shadowed The Lost Estate's production *The Great Christmas Feast*. She is particularly interested in physical theatre where small details have a big impact.

Liverpool's theatres, Sparking Creativity and Nurturing Talent

Rooted in Liverpool's spirit, the Everyman & Playhouse are a creative powerhouse with national and international impact, driven by a passion for theatre, the city, and the belief that theatre can entertain, inspire and fuel positive social change.

With two distinctive venues, each rich in history, they offer unforgettable experiences that captivate the imagination and ignite curiosity. Producing local stories with national impact, they champion emerging talent, innovative storytelling and breathe new life into the classics. Liverpool Everyman & Playhouse want to be the most exciting places to experience and create theatre.

A registered charity (1081229), the theatres acknowledge the continued support of Arts Council England and Liverpool City Council, and their audiences, donors, patrons and partners. For audiences, artists, and communities alike, Liverpool Everyman & Playhouse are places of wonder, magic, and extraordinary moments waiting for you to enjoy.

everymanplayhouse.com

 @livEveryPlay  /everymanplayhouse

FOR THE EVERYMAN & PLAYHOUSE

THANK YOU

Liverpool Everyman & Playhouse are a registered charity (1081229) and gratefully acknowledge the support of our funders, donors, patrons, partners and audiences.

For their ongoing financial support, we would like to thank

Alder Hey Children's Charity, Art Friends Merseyside, The Austin and Hope Pilkington Trust, Backstage Trust, Cameron Mackintosh Foundation, The Foyle Foundation, Garfield Weston Foundation, The Granada Foundation, The Helena Trust, The Hemby Charitable Trust, The Idlewild Trust, Lady Anne Dodd, The Low Carbon Eco, Innovatory Fund*, The Parr Group, The Steel Charitable Trust

Our Major Partner
Brabners

Our Higher Education Partner
Liverpool Hope University

Our Business Members & Sponsors
Bruntwood, Duncan Sheard Glass, Liverpool Growth Platform, Liverpool & Sefton Chamber of Commerce, Open Media, Professional Liverpool, Red Hat Consulting, Warwick North West, Wirral Chamber of Commerce, Wrightsure Insurance Group

Our Hotel Partners
Hope Street Hotel and School Lane Hotel

Our Alumni Supporters
Jim Broadbent, Matthew Kelly, Sir Ian McKellen, David Morrissey, Bill Nighy, Eddie Redmayne, Willy Russell, Alison Steadman, Julie Walters

Our Patrons
Alan Sprince, Lara and Richie Pearn, John and Mary Belchem, Robin Bloxsidge and Nick Riddle, John Birkenhead, Cath and Phil Kightley, J Mason, Lorraine and Steve Groves, Andrea Nixon and Dan Stinson, Owen Jones, Jim McKenna

Those who have left a Legacy or an In Memory Gift
Alan Harkness Lewis, Anni Parker & Brian Barry lovers and supporters of theatre

Dorothy Smellie, Fanchon Frolich, Malcolm & Roger Frood in memory of Graham & Joan Frood, Michael Key, The Dunham Family in loving memory of Matthew Dunham, Board Member and friend

And to everyone who gives monthly or annually for their continued support, and to all who supported the new Everyman Ev4Ev campaign, our Young Everyman Playhouse appeal in 2022/23, and our Everyone Starts Somewhere campaign in 2024/25

*LCEI is funded by the UK Government through the UK Shared Prosperity Fund, with the Liverpool City Region Combined Authority as the lead authority

ATTACHMENT

A new play by Julia Cranney

For every family who has experience of the UK's care system

CAST

Mat *(30s) a scouser, a loner, an only child.*

NOTES

( ) are thoughts, not spoken aloud.

Spacing is used to indicate pacing and rhythm.

GLITCH*s vary in intensity and length but they are always moments where Mat is pulled back into the present tense of NOW. Sometimes they are welcome, sometimes they are not.*

The voices of other people are heard throughout the play, sometimes Mat speaks them, sometimes we hear them.

NOW

Mat's *stood by herself. Holding a well-worn twelve- to eighteen-
month old baby boy's jumper.*

It isn't even a big stain.

       Is it?

This morning I thought it was massive and I didn't have
time to soak it. But. How long would it take to get that off
there? Two minutes? It's yoghurt. It's not . . .

But this morning. We didn't – We didn't have two minutes.
So I just –

And now he doesn't have it. And they're going to say it
doesn't matter. But –

We're suddenly pulled out of this moment into somewhere else:

1

It's raining. Hard.

I shouldn't be here.

I should be wearing my pyjamas. The baggy ones with the white dots. And I should have something shit on the telly and I should be warm. But instead, I'm fighting with my umbrella at a random bus stop because the 53 got diverted and kicked us all off. And now obviously I have no idea what time the next bus is going to arrive because someone's written 'This bus stop fucked your mum' over the timetable. And this day –

I don't think days can get shitter than this.

Because everything's gone wrong. Today. Right from first thing this morning. Before I was even dressed. Before I was even dressed I'd written today off. Because I was meant to have a shower this morning but the water. It wasn't hot. It was cold. There was – Sometimes my boiler does this thing where it just. Stops fucking working.

For twelve hours at a time and, yeah.

It did that this morning. So I was cold from before I woke up and then I couldn't have a proper shower – And it doesn't feel the same, does it? Having a cold wash in the sink. Even though I used soap. (Obviously I used soap.)

I just felt.

Like you could smell me.

Not a bad smell. Not really. But a *smell*. So I've just. Not wanted to move. All day.

Not that I move a lot. Behind the counter. I try to always stay behind the counter. At a distance. Because. Well because you don't linger in a pharmacy. You get in and you get out. Especially the mums. The mums are on a mission. Desperate for calpol or vitamins, nit shampoo. They're always carrying screaming babies strapped to their chest or pushing grotty toddlers in buggies who look sturdy enough to kick the shit out of anyone who asks them for a bit of their sausage roll.

So I'd spent all day. Like this. (Holding my arms like this.) Looking at the clock. Waiting for it to be home time. To get back home. To my flat. To get a proper wash and – just. Breathe.

But then there was this one mum. Today. Who came in at five to six. I'd already cashed up. Mr Boggiani had gone home. I should have been going home. But she came in wanting care of the chemist. For her baby. But he had worms, she said. He wasn't himself. He couldn't settle. She needed medicine now. And I told her there wasn't anything I could do. That the pharmacist was gone. She'd have to come back in the morning.

But she just kept asking me to look at him. How wriggly he was. And I could see him fine. From where I was standing. He looked like a ham. But she kept getting closer – Telling me to look. *Really look*. Leaning across the counter. Like she wanted to hand him to me or something. Like she wanted me to pick him up and hold him in my hands. Hold this *baby* that I don't even know. And he was wriggling then. In the air. And it was past closing and she wouldn't stop so I just –

Gave her the bottle of Ovex.

Threw it to her. Said it was on the house. And she took it – Didn't say thank you. But left me to lock up. Sanitise my hands. And then as soon as I stepped outside I could see my bus leaving. Which meant a thirty-five-minute wait in the rain.

Only to end up here. Diverted to a different part of St Helens.

At a bus stop that doesn't even have a bus stop.

Mat *is suddenly doused in water.*

It's a skoda. A fucking dickhead in a fucking skoda – Because of *course* it is. Anybody else would have been able to see the massive fucking puddle – Anybody else who's driven past the bus stop in the last twenty minutes *has* managed to avoid driving straight through the middle of the massive fucking puddle – But this – bellend has nearly fucking drowned me. And he has the audacity to stop when I shout at him?

He's reversing. He's reversing back towards me and I'm going to really let him have it. Because today's been a long day. Today's been a really long day and this is just – I'm going to let him have it and scream in his fucking (face) –

But then he asks me if I want a lift.

And I know that's a bad idea. My nan would kill me. She'd have killed me if I told her that I got in a car with a strange man. She was always telling me – 'Never get in a car with a strange man', which was weird, because how many times do you ever actually end up in a situation where you *might* get into a car with a strange man anyway? That's what I used to say. Like, as if I would, if I had any choice in the matter. But then – he had a face like a dog. A sad but gorgeous dog – and he looked so warm and kind that – I don't know.

I blinked. And then I'd said yes and I was inside and he was apologising again, but loads, and turning on the heated seat – He turned it on and then kept asking if it was OK – 'the heated seat' – like he was sorry but also wanted me to be a bit impressed by the fact his dead old car that had just soaked me in stagnant water had a heated seat – And somehow him doing that wasn't annoying it was – cute? In a tragic way, maybe. But cute. And he told a joke that was shit and I didn't even think I was really listening but then I heard myself laughing. And it wasn't the fake laugh that I use all day at work when a customer says something stupid, but it was my real laugh. My real laugh from deep down in my belly and it's been so long since I heard it that I'd almost forgotten it was there – But there it was. And it was nice. And he's nice. And he tells me his name is James. And I tell him I'm Mat.

And he doesn't ask me if that's short for anything, he just repeats it with a bit of a smile. And then we're outside my flat and it feels like twenty-seven minutes took twenty-seven seconds, so I ask him if he wants to come inside – Of my flat – For a bit. And I'm blushing, which is fucking stupid because I'm thirty-two years old. But it doesn't matter. And he says yes.

GLITCH

When it's done, we hear the thumping loud noise of a soft play centre:

I don't like kids. Even when I was a kid I didn't like kids.

And this place is *full* of kids.

I used to love these types of places. When I was little. I mean – I only ever went to one. Jungle Bungle on the East Lancs – basically a shed with a ball pool in it next door to a pub that my nan's mate Kev worked in. But there were tunnels and a big yellow slide and you could sort of climb back behind the netting and squeeze into the tiniest little crawl space which was perfect for hide and seek. Which I liked because then you didn't have to talk to any of the other kids. Who I never knew. Because I never really knew anyone for that long. And you don't ask people their names at the jungle bungle. You just sort of – join in. If they let you. So I used to climb inside the net. I'd climb inside the net and wait there for ages. And nobody would normally find me, because they wouldn't be looking. But my heart would be thumping. And the few times – The few times that someone was looking – because they were really looking for their brother or sister or their cousin or whatever – But the few times that someone was looking and they found *me*, I'd get so excited that I'd just run.

I'd run so fast so far and so fast, round and round. Up and down and round and down that slide that was too small but also too fast and back up again. I'd be dripping in sweat and my heart would be thumping and then I'd burst into tears when my nan made me come out to drink my slush and eat my curly fries.

But this place is (different). It's massive. There's a climbing wall and a football pitch and six different slides. It actually makes me feel a bit sick, how tall it is. Like – four flights of stairs tall. If a kid snuck out of that netting and they were at the top they'd just – die. Fully die. Like, splat.

> And it doesn't feel very responsible.
> Just – letting them do it.

But what do I know about what's responsible?

We were meant to pick Grace up from Helen's at nine this morning. And I overslept.

> I mean, I didn't. I woke up at half five.
> Four. It was early.

I tried to go back to sleep but I couldn't because James was snoring a bit and I kept thinking that he'd stopped breathing when he stopped snoring for a second so I decided to go downstairs and catch up on EastEnders and plan what I was going to say when we got there. But then I fell asleep and James woke me up because it was 8:45 and I was still in my pyjamas and it was only when we were sitting in the skoda that I couldn't remember if I'd brushed my teeth. I mean, I know I did. I always do brush my teeth. But I couldn't remember doing it *this* morning so I got James to stop at the mini tescos on the way. To buy some mints. And we were only a few minutes late to pick her up. But they weren't in.

> Or that's what Helen said. On speaker phone. In the
> car. This morning, when she didn't know I was
> listening –

She said we were late and she can't put my life on hold for – whatever this is.

Whatever this is. She said that. Like she doesn't know. Like she thinks that I'm . . . That I'm not someone to be taken seriously. With James. Because why would she take me seriously, really? I mean I get it – It's been fast. I said that. To James. When he first whispered it in my ear.

James Do you think you're ready to meet Grace?

And I said No.

> No. No. No. Straight away. Because well. Because we hadn't even been seeing each other that long.

> Six months.

And six months sounds like half a year. Because it is half a year. And half a year feels like a big chunk of time really, doesn't it? If you're spending it together. If you realise that you're both making the journey to St Helens every day. It makes sense, doesn't it? To spend that time. In the morning and in the afternoon. Together.

And there's a part of me that worries maybe it's all because of that? The not having to get the bus from mine into town, and then another one from town back out again until it gets to St Helens.

> And James' car is quite nice really.

But if it was just about the car. Then you wouldn't spend – all of the other time. Together too. Would you? And you wouldn't be bothered if he – if he didn't reply to your message for fourteen hours. Or whatever amount of time. If he didn't reply to a message one time, it wouldn't make you feel sick. Like he was just – suddenly gone or whatever. Vanished out of nowhere.

Because James would never vanish out of nowhere. He's. He's the most solidly – solid person. Just. He's just there. Really. I mean, he's not perfect. He's –

When I first stayed over at his he said he just needed to change the sheets and he pulled a full duvet, with the covers on and pillows, out of the cupboard – And swapped them over.

He didn't wash them.

Just.

Swapped them.

And he thought that was changing the sheets.

I thought it was a joke – You think it's a joke. He's an attractive man – Not being funny – He is, he's an attractive man. He used to be a married man. He's a dad, but he thought that that was OK. Genuinely. Something about keeping the sheets in a cold room and freshness or – I don't know. Something mad.

But I still found myself wanting to – To spend all my time with him. Once I'd got him to buy new bedding. Obviously. And put it on a proper wash. Hung it outside to dry.

And I wanted – I want to make him happy. So when I said no, about meeting Grace – I could see – I could see that that wasn't what he wanted me to say. And something just –

Something just made me say yes. Which made him beam. And that made me feel like – Obviously yes was the answer. Yes was always the answer.

But then this morning. When I was sat in the car. In the cold. With no Grace. Watching James stood outside on the phone, trying to reason with Helen. That felt really fucking stupid.

And we were only ten minutes late but they were gone. No answer. Nobody was in.

And I think even if we hadn't been late, she'd have done the same.

Left. Cos she's always doing stuff like that with James. Even though she was the one that left him in the first place. And that was *years* ago. She's nasty.

But there's no point saying anything because I know James doesn't want to argue with her.

He never will. Says it's not worth it.

So he just asks her what she wants him to do.

And she says that she's sorry but there's nothing she can do because she has to take *the boys* to their five a side – The boys are her boyfriend's sons.

Kenny, Gerrard and Ynwa – It's not Welsh. It's an acronym. For You'll Never Walk Alone.

– I know

It's a really important match apparently. They can't be late. It's not professional.

And if I was James I'd have been shouting at this point. But James just does that sucking in his breath thing he does when he's feeling a bit stressed.

And I've fucked it. I've definitely fucked it. We're not seeing Grace today.

And it makes me feel guilty thinking it. But part of me (a big part) just wants James to tell Helen to forget all about it.

Then we could stop (sitting in this guilt) and go back home. To his flat. Just the two of us. And that would probably be better. Wouldn't it? For the best.

But before I could say that James rings his dad. Who just – listens and says he'll sort it.

The soft play noise is back.

So that's how I met Gareth. James' dad. At soft play. He *is* Welsh. And funny. And meeting Gareth I understand why James is the way he is. Because why would you ever be nervous to meet anyone if your dad is Gareth? He's just. Sunshine. In a dad or grandad. Bamps. That's what Grace calls him. He gave me a massive hug and said I could call him whatever I liked so long as I kept his son smiling like he has been. He was so – sunshine-y that I hardly even clocked Grace. She was holding his hand the whole time. Even when he was hugging me.

I told her I liked her hair.

I'd read that you're not really supposed to do that anymore. When you meet little girls. That's what the mumsnet thread said. That I was reading this morning. It said you shouldn't comment on how girls look. You should ask them what they want to be when they grow up, but honestly I think that's a bit intense – And her hair was amazing. All ginger and curly and down to her bum and she smiled and looked a bit shy and said that her mum makes her have it in plaits if she's not straightened it, but Bamps let her take them out in the car because they were too tight.

And I said I can't deal with things that feel tight on my head either. That's why I have my hair like this.

She said I looked like a mermaid.

And that was that –

We just sort of – Went off into the soft play together.

And it's sticky. It's got sticky bits where there shouldn't be sticky bits. It all needs a bleach. A proper good bleach with a proper good cloth. But when Grace laughs her nose does this thing that James' does when he laughs – So I just focus on that. On her nose when she laughs. And making it happen again.

She's smart and funny and six years old but she makes me laugh like nobody's business. We took her to McDonald's after and she said that her mum says girls shouldn't eat McDonald's so I buy her a milkshake and a mcflurry to go with her happy meal and I have a happy meal too which makes her laugh and the three of us all eat on the floor of

James' living room, with a beach towel spread out under us like a picnic blanket.

And when we're finished we decide to watch Strictly – Which I don't normally go in for but Grace wants to be a dancer, so she gets all snuggly with her dad under the brown blanket on the sofa and I'm sitting on the chair when she lifts up the blanket and asks me to sit next to her. So I do. And then she just plonks her legs on my legs. Without thinking about it. Without asking. And she smiles. And we watch Strictly.

GLITCH

So that's our thing now. Gareth picks her up on a Saturday, and we do an activity – Soft Play or the museum or going to Sefton Park. And then we have a McDonald's on the floor and watch Strictly and she sleeps over. And all of a sudden, Strictly's over, it's the Christmas Special and me and James do Christmas together for the first time. Which is nice. And quiet. Because I don't really go in for the whole Christmas thing – Not since I've been by myself. But I come home from work and there, and he's got – The Muppets Christmas Carol blasting out of the speakers and he's at the top of a ladder next to this tree that is – Honestly it's bigger than the ceiling. I don't even know how he got it up the stairs. And he says that he wants to do every Christmas with me.

Grace comes to her dad's on boxing day and she's only meant to be staying 'til the twenty-seventh but we text and ask if she can stay for a couple of days. Which is mad. Because there hadn't been any proper planning. But Helen says yes and Grace's nose does the thing. And it's nice. But then when she goes back. To her mum's. It's – horrible. Not having her there. In the house –

It feels empty. And I should be going to my flat. I haven't been there since Christmas eve but – It feels wrong. Leaving James on his own. When we've been a three that long – So I ask him. If this year. If we can be living together. I don't even think about it. The words just sort of come out of my mouth. Because of course we should be living together. Shouldn't we?

James Yeah

He says

James Yeah I'd really love that Mat.

So yeah – That's it basically.

Mat *smiles.*

But I'm having a bit of a problem. With the cleaning.

Before James – I used to do a mini clean on a Tuesday – Sometimes Wednesday – and a big one on Sunday. Properly. Getting on my hands and knees, doing the skirting boards. Polishing with Mr Sheen. I've got different cloths for different rooms. Like my nan did. And the way I divide it up – If I just stick to the schedule, little one on Tuesday – Sometimes Wednesday – big one on Sunday, and the colours. It's fine. It's nice.

I mean, I'm not one of those people who get off on it. When I was a teenager I used to hate it. I didn't understand why we had to do it twice a week – And that's not counting the mopping and hoovering and sink wipe downs every day. And I'm not like my nan with that now, I don't vacuum every day. I mean I wipe down the sink. But the cleans. I just do the little clean on Tuesday and the big clean on Sunday. And that keeps on top of things. It keeps your mind tidy. That's what Barb said. Tidy house, tidy mind. *There's no excuse to be living in filth.* That's what she'd say. If she saw this. Now.

> And I know this is not filthy. Obviously – I mean, look at it.

But since we moved in – I've been skipping the Tuesday. Putting it off to Wednesday – Then Thursday or Friday and suddenly its Sunday and I might as well just roll it into one. Do it all on the one day. But I know that's not the way to do it. Because then you fall behind on the washing. And not just of the clothes – But the cloths. So you don't have the right cloth colours for the right rooms and – And I sound mental.

I know I sound mental. James says I don't sound mental, but I haven't spoken to him about it as much as I (think about it). I've just told him that I like to look after my house in a certain way and that I can't do it if we're always – together. You know?

And I thought for a second he was going to dump me – My heart was going so fast and wanted to be sick. I wanted to just. Swallow the words back up. Pretend that I'd never said them in the first place.

But then he just smiled and said OK. Said he'd give me some space. Not come home 'til bedtime.

And when he'd left, on that first Tuesday. I felt a bit sad. That he was gone. And then I was fucking made up because I could *blitz* the place. Properly. Take all the furniture away from the walls and clean out the fridge and scrub down the inside of the microwave. I did so much that I was thinking I should call it a night, go to bed – but then I thought, the bathroom won't take me long. I can do that. Then the whole house has been done. Top to bottom. On a *Tuesday*.

So that's how we've been doing it. Every Tuesday. And on Sunday mornings Grace gets involved too. With the dusting. She likes the dusting. And she makes her bed in the mornings, shows me how neat it is. Dead proud. And so am I. Because this – This is working, isn't it? We've got a rhythm.

I still haven't met her. Helen. She basically refuses to even acknowledge I exist.

But Grace comes here every Wednesday for an overnight. And then every Friday til Sunday. That's the basics – But sometimes it just makes sense for her to stay longer. Because the boys have competitions. All over the country. And Helen has to take them, and that's not really fair on Grace –

making her traipse to all of those places in the cold. In the
summer it might be different. But I don't think it will.
Because we just have a nice time – The three of us.

We have a nice time. Most of the time. I mean – Grace has an
amazing time. We do painting and drawing and baking.
Glitter, glue, papier (mâché) or whatever the fuck it's called
with the newspapers. Nano tape. If you can picture it, we've
done it. We do it. And it's everywhere. Like, everywhere. Not
just little piles or bits and pieces on the kitchen table. But the
whole house. The whole house is starting to look like B and
M has exploded in it but James and Grace – They don't see
mess. It's not there in front of them. Unless it's in their way,
and then they might – shove it in a cupboard or pile it up on
a chair and I – It makes my skin itch a bit. Not literally. But
(sort of –) Sometimes – Sometimes I feel like I need to lie
down in a room with nothing and nobody in it for a bit. Only
I know if I did that. They'd come and lie down next to me.

> And that's cute, isn't it? It's lovely. The way
> they both just – Say what they're feeling.

> All the time.

> 'I love you' I love you I love you. Ten times a minute
> sometimes. It's just. Different.

I loved my nan and my nan loved me but we weren't like.

> Every five minutes. (It's different.) But that's OK.
> That's just them. And this is us now.

GLITCH

One night we were on the sofa, watching something on telly.
And we were meant to be dropping her off back at Helen's
once it finished. But when the credits started she went all
quiet and stiff. And didn't want to tell us what's wrong.
Which isn't like Grace. But eventually, she tells us she doesn't
want to go back to her mum's.

And there's a part of me that's happy when she says that. A big part. But I see James' face and it's crushed. So then I feel like a dickhead. Obviously you can't want her not to want to go home. That's her home. We ask what the matter is. And she takes a while to start. But once she does she can't stop talking.

She says that the boys don't like her. That they're loud and mean and noisy. They're so noisy that sometimes she feels like she can't think. She wishes that she never had to go there.

James says she doesn't really mean what she's saying. Lots of kids are noisy. She loves the boys – They're like her brothers. But she's insistent. They're *not*. Because they don't want to be. They've said so.

I ask her if that's what she wants – For them to be her brothers. Maybe that's it.

But she's positive that that is absolutely not it. She doesn't want *them* to be her brothers. But she does want a brother. Or a sister. A real one. That if me and her dad had a baby that would be amazing.

> And I don't know where to look. Or what to say. But I can feel James looking at for me for ages.

And in the end he just laughs. So Grace laughs too and James gets her to get her coat on, promises that we can do an extra sleepover this week. Says that her mum will miss her if she doesn't go. And she'll miss her mum. I get ready to go with them but he looks at me and says it's fine – Why don't I run myself a bath?

So I do. When he's gone. I run the bath. Fill it all the way up. Use some of the bright pink bubbles we'd bought for Grace. Get in.

And it hits me.

> I fucking hate baths. Always have. Don't know why I
> thought it'd be different – I just – I don't know. It
> was something to do.

Somewhere to think, for forty seconds, before getting back
out. Wrapping myself in a towel. Having a look in the mirror.

Maybe Grace is right. I don't know. Maybe she's not. But –
I've never wanted – this – before. Never really imagined.
Actually having a – family. Because it never seemed real. For
me. Too far away and –

I –   I think I want to do it.

                Or I think I want to want to do it.

And when James gets home. He says he wants to do it too.

So we do.

And again. And again. And again – I mean – You get the
picture.

At first we just – I just stop taking the pill. We're not really
trying, trying – Just. We're not, not trying. And I think for a
few days that maybe – It's already happened.

But that's fucking stupid because then my period comes.
Bang on. Early actually. Two days early. That's how fucking
not pregnant I am.

And the months keep coming. And so does the bleeding.
Bang on track. Every time. And that starts to hurt.
Obviously. Obviously it starts to hurt. I've been told since I
was twelve years old that I was one shit shag away from a
baby I don't want but now. Now that I actually want a baby to
show up – It just – *doesn't*.

        And it's hard not to think that that's a sign.

I've spent my whole life saying I don't want one. My body's
heard that. It's taken it on board it – You can't just totally
turn your mind upside down about something like that and

expect it to just – happen. That's what I tell myself. I just need to – wait it out.

James says maybe it's time we start doing it properly. Which is what I thought we were doing. But obviously we're not.

We download an app. And get sticks to pee on – And I lie with my legs in the air afterwards – James reads an article about the power of positive mental attitudes so I get rid of my tampons. Decide this month is going to be the month. And then end up having to make a late night trek to the corner shop.

It's months of that. Months.

Nothing changes.

Then one day I go to the cathedral. Which is insane.

I've not been there since school. But I'm getting the bus into town and it just – I see the street sign. And I think maybe I'll just pop in. Light a candle. What harm can it do? So I do. And then when I'm finished I panic because I can't remember if Nan was Catholic or not. Because she was into all that when she was little. Not after. Not with (my mum) or with me. But I got them to do the last rites, in the hospital, when she (died). And that priest was a woman – If she was a priest? And if she was she wasn't a Catholic. So I decided to walk down the street to the other one. It feels like it's going to rain the whole way but it doesn't. Until the second I get there. Then it buckets down. Just as I walk through the gate. And I'm soaked. I'm so wet I don't think I'll be able to light a candle. But I do.

And when I've finished I sit under the neon sign. Just to dry off. That's what I say I'm doing. In my head. But it's quiet in that church-y? cathedral-y? way where it's quiet but loud with thoughts or whatever. So I sit there. Thinking. And I ask. In my head. I ask whoever there is out there – If its G-d or Buddha or my nan or whatever. To just – Give us a hand. Let us be a family.

And I swear to God I feel something twinge. Here. And obviously that sounds mad. I know that. But. I don't know. I did. I felt something. It felt like someone was listening.

They weren't.

Four days later I text James on his way home. Ask him to get a box of tampax, the cheapest bottle of red he can find and a straw.

I try to laugh it off.

But when I see him. I crumple. It's like a wave of sad just – Knocks me over.

There's nothing funny to say.

Because this is shit.

Proper shit.

And I don't know how we're supposed to keep going. Running headfirst down a tunnel convinced that there's going to be light somewhere at the end of it, but it just keeps getting longer and longer.

Darker and darker.

Then that night. Under the covers – He whispers in my ear.

James Do you want to talk about trying something different?

I tell him – I don't think tonight's the night for trying a different position dickhead. And he laughs. We both laugh. My laugh was a bit snotty. But it was a laugh.

And I don't want to do IVF. I tell him that I don't think I can. I don't think I can put my body – My brain through that – Pressure. And he says we could think about adoption, couldn't we?

And he's not – We've never really. Talked about that – Not properly. I mean. We watched that documentary. The one everyone was watching. Last year. About the ginger family that adopts that other family with all the blonde kids. And seeing them do that, for them. It just. It really got to me and he'd seen that and he'd squeezed my feet and said. We could do that. One day. If we want to.

But I thought – I didn't think he meant it literally. I thought we'd want to – I thought he'd want us to do it the real way first. But he says

James   Any way that ends with us having a family is the real way.

And I love him. I love him so much. Right then. Right now. There's nothing about this man that I don't love. And he's right. Obviously, he's right. Apart from the bit that ends with us having a family. Because we are one. Already. We're more family than I've ever had. We're a family now and we're going to find someone else to join us. Because that would be amazing. What could be better than that?

GLITCH

2

Getting ready to adopt is like training for a marathon. I think. I've never trained for a marathon. But if it involves a fuck ton of people poking and prodding you. Asking you to tell them all of your deepest darkest secrets and memories. And insisting that you have a spare bedroom. It's exactly like training for a marathon.

We called them the next morning. The local council. I'd stayed up after James fell asleep. Couldn't close my eyes. Too fizzed up with – ideas. So I'd researched. And there was a meeting for prospective adoptees that Friday – Which felt like a sign, right? That being so easy?

But that was the last easy thing about it, to be honest. Which is fine. I mean. This isn't something to fuck up, is it? This is something that you need to get right. Or – Well, you don't want to get it wrong. You need to be honest.

But I wasn't. Honest. On the phone that morning. When they were taking our details. When they asked me if I had a spare room. I lied. I'll admit that. When they asked me on the phone that first day, I lied. And looking back now – I don't think that was a real make or break question. But it felt like it. So when they asked me. I said yes. And now we do.

> Even though we basically just made the spare room by getting Gareth to board out the loft.

> We wouldn't put a kid in the loft.

They want references. From work – Mr Boggiani says he'll do it for fifty quid at first but then he laughs and he never asks for it again so I'm pretty sure he was joking. And they want a personal reference – but I'm not sure who to go for for that. And then I remember Ifeoma. She lived next door to Nan. The whole time, from before I'd moved in. And when Nan got sick Ifeoma would drop off these big dinners on Fridays that would last us through the week. She did that every week for three years. And when I realise it was three years, I feel a bit guilty that I've left it so long since I last saw her. So I send her a message on Facebook. Which she fucking loves – Facebook. I mean, she's all over it. But she loves the message too. Hearts it. Replies straight away. Like she was waiting for it. And we speak on the phone. She's over the moon when I tell her what we need. Says it's no problem at all. That Barb would have been thrilled –

Which I guess she would have been.

It's trickier with James. Not the work or the personal references. That's easy. Obviously. James has loads of friends. Everyone loves James. But because he's already a dad. They want to talk to Grace's mum. They want to talk to Helen. Which is a nightmare.

I know it's going to be a nightmare. I tell our social worker Sarah that it's going to be a nightmare. Sarah meets Grace. Of course Sarah meets Grace, and she's happy about that, they have quite a few little chats, but that's not enough – She has to talk to Helen.

And I'm pulling my hair out, trying to get James to get Helen to commit to a date. Not even to meet Sarah in person – Because she says that she's too busy to do that. Just to talk to her on the computer. But she keeps cancelling.

And I just know. I just know in my bones that this is going to be the thing. The thing in the back of my head. That I've been waiting for. Because that's what happens, isn't it? You get everything ready. You do everything right. Try your best. But if you're not (– lucky). Well then none of it matters, does it.

GLITCH

I'm 'resilient'.

That's what they say about me. In the information gathering sessions. Which we do every week. Sat next to each other on the sofa in the living room. Or the kitchen table. Answering questions about what I've been through. Before my nan. It's made me *resilient*. And I am. (I think.)

We have to go to classes too.

And I was no good at school but *this*. The classes. This I'm good at. You don't get ranked at it. But if you did. If there was a ranking. Top. It'd be me. Any extra session. Any tick box. I'm in. The advanced first aid and the trauma informed parenting, the early permanence sessions and even the ARFID information seminar. You give me information about how to do this. Do this well. And I'm going to take it in, memorise it. And know it. In my bones.

I've got a folder – I've actually got three different folders. And a stack of books that the social workers have mentioned. You don't have to read all the books, but I get them second hand online and I make notes in the margins. Copy them out onto pieces of paper. File them, organise them. And it's there. Perfect. Ready to go.

It's not just talking though. You have to write down . . . Everything. There's this booklet you have to fill in. Before you can go to the next stage. You have to do that as well as the classes and –

The booklet . . . The booklet's taking me a bit longer.

James' bit is finished. He's done. I say he's done, but if we're really honest, I wrote most of his answers. He told me what to say. But I filled it in. And his is just right now. I got Gareth to help me with the family tree you have to put in. You only need to go back to grand-parents but I did great grand-parents for him too. On both sides.

(Mine's much smaller.)

There's this question 'Describe your childhood in at least 2,000 to 4,000 words by providing examples that will illustrate your childhood experiences'.

And James' easy. It's a piece of piss. Gareth and his mam and his aunties – He has loads of aunties. The first boy in a long line of girls – On both sides. The first grandchild. He always says that: *The First Grandchild.*

And that's me too. I was the first grandchild. But it's not . . . I don't want to write that. On mine. I don't want to write anything.

They say that doing this stuff, writing it all down, talking about it, that it'll bring up things about ourselves. That it's hard. But I'm *resilient.* And it's not hard. Because I know what I want: Them not to say no.

James keeps asking me to read what I've done. Says maybe that I'm too *close* to it. He'll do it for me. But that's stupid because his spelling is shit and he'd get it wrong and I just . . .

Don't want to write it down.

I've spoken about it. To our social worker – To Sarah. I can speak about it. Sat next to James. But if I write it down. He'll read it and then he'll look at me in my eyes. And I don't mind it in the (context) in the world of getting them to say yes. But I don't actually want to talk about it with James. Don't want him to dig through it like he does.

Not in a mean way – But. I don't want it to be in our house.

My childhood started when I was nine. That sounds weird and I know it sounds weird. But that's when it started. Before then (I didn't really have one). I know that I should have lots of memories before then. But I don't. So I can't just – Make them up for the sake of a form?

And I keep getting emails from Sarah. Asking me if I've finished – She says it doesn't need to be perfect. Like *that's* what I'm worrying about.

> And then there's a note at the end saying that she still hasn't managed to get hold of Helen.

So that morning I tell James – I tell him that he has to pull his finger out. Get Helen to get involved. Properly.

But he looks at me and says –

James Do you think it's worth it?

And I feel like my heart's fallen out. Just. Doof. Onto the floor.

> Because he doesn't want to do this. Does he?

> Of course he doesn't.

> And I can't look at him.

> So I start walking.

Straight out the door. James wanted to come after me but Gareth was about to drop off Grace and I just. Didn't stop. Kept walking.

And all of it's swimming through my body. Making my hands tingle. I'm sad. Really proper sad. But also I'm *angry*. Because this is – This is Helen's fault isn't it?

We were on a roll. We were ready to go and then – Then she just. Wouldn't fucking do what we needed her to. This woman, who won't even *lower herself* to meeting me and I just think: No. No fucking way.

So I walk to her house. On the new build estate. With its big red door and the penalty shoot out goal in the front. And I get ready. As I'm walking up the path. Looking at the perfect borders and the perfect grass. I can feel my blood (fizzing). That whirling feeling in my neck. I'm gonna stay calm. I tell myself I'm gonna stay calm. But looking at the perfect house with her perfect boys – Who aren't even her boys. I just hammer on the door.

And she doesn't know who I am. I can see on her face when she answers the door, she has no idea who I am. She's just looking at me. Confused.

And all of a sudden I just. Couldn't catch my breath. I was
breathing so hard but none of it was air. And I felt like this
was it. This was going to be how I go. How it ends – Shouting
at a woman who doesn't even recognise me. Doesn't realise
she's got my whole world in her hands. And I'm *angry*. I'm
raging. I'm so angry I can't breathe –

And she tells me to

Helen Stop. Slow down. Take deep breaths. You're gonna
be alright.

When it passes. I'm sat in her kitchen with my head between
my legs. And I'm so embarrassed that I don't want to sit up.
Don't want to look her in the face. And she – Senses it? I
think. Says I don't have to rush. But that she's got to pick up
the boys, so I can just close the door after me, when I'm
feeling better. And she leaves. Says

Helen It was nice to finally meet you Mat.

That's what she said. And it didn't even sound like she was
lying. So I said nothing. Just. Waited to hear her car drive
away. Then I picked myself up. And walked out.

And it was dark by the time I got back. Grace was in bed.
And I hovered by the door. Not knowing if I wanted to go in.

But then James opened it. And he looked at me.

And I looked at him.

And it all came flooding out. Helen and her kitchen and the
form. How I couldn't do the form. How I couldn't put it into
the right words. How they were running round my head all
the time but I couldn't – How do you write all that down in
2,000 words that make sense *and* make them want to say yes
to what we want. And it doesn't even matter did it? Because
he doesn't want this. He didn't even want to go to Helen, did
he? He doesn't want any of it. Because he'd realised that this
was all a big mistake.

And he didn't say anything. Just looked at me. In the doorway.

>So I said I'd just grab a bag. Of my things.

And then he got hold of me, gentle – But *there*. On my shoulders. Both hands.

And he called me a gobshite.

>And I couldn't – I couldn't register anything. Just the feeling of his hands on my shoulders and the way his mouth was smiling, but his eyes were worried and said

James   Of course I want this. I thought *you* didn't want this anymore.

And then I was crying. Which is mad. Because I don't cry. But I was crying.

And James just held me. Didn't tell me to stop.

But when I did, he said we'd write the form together. Tonight. And we stayed up 'til three.

>Writing it all down.

>It wasn't all of it. But it was honest. And that'll do. Won't it?

GLITCH

Not long after sending the form, James got a message from Helen. Just a short one. And it said that she'd do what we needed. Then after that we were flying.

And in no time we were going to panel. Which made me feel so nervous I felt like my stomach was going to fall out of my mouth. But it didn't.

We just answered the questions. In this big room. With these nine serious faces. They were all questions that we'd done before with Sarah – What's the process been like? How will

Grace cope with a sibling? What do you think are the challenges you might face as an adoptive parent?

But then the chair – She asked me a question from a list she had, that some kids in care had given her. A list of questions that they wanted prospective adopters to be asked. And I thought it'd be really heavy. Sad, or – But it was:

What will we do as a family that will be fun?

And I said –

> we'll do so much.

> We'll do so so much that's fun. Parks and museums and dance classes. Pizza pyjama parties where we put music on and dance, watching bad movies and eating ice cream and big birthday discos – If that's what they want – but we'll also do the other stuff. The stuff that's not so fun when you first think about it, like homework or the little clean on Tuesday and the big clean on Sunday. But that will be fun. Because we'll be together. We'll be together forever and that will be the most fun in the world. I promise.

Later in the car, James took the mick out of my fun answer, said it sounded like something out of a Hallmark movie – And he'll tell Grace on Wednesday when she's saying that she's bored doing her times tables that what she really means is that she's having *fun*. But I just call him a twat and smile like my face is going to fall off.

Because they approved us and everything's going right. Everything's going to work.

Everything's looking like it's going to work –

A longer pause – then **GLITCH**.

Nobody expects to get life changing news when they're wearing a wonder woman costume. But that's what happened to us. Grace had been invited to a Hallowe'en party with some girls from school. And it was superhero themed, which is cute, obviously. But the day before the little girl's mum texted us to check that we'd seen that parents were supposed to dress up too – It'll be *fun*. That's what she said. Fun.

Will it? I don't like fancy dress. It takes me ages to buy clothes that I like that are just for me – Buying a costume is – well it's asking for trouble. And the party was less than twenty-four hours away and Grace was excited so I just. Order one online. Same day delivery. Which I can never really wrap my head around. But it arrives. Bang on time. Eight o'clock that night. One for me and one for James. But mine's awful. When I opened the packet it looked like it was Grace's size. But there wasn't time to get anything else so I just – closed my ears and pulled it up. Put my flannel shirt over the top. Which sort of spoiled the look but there was nothing to be done. We had to get out the door. The three of us dressed in knock-off lycra.

And then the phone rang.

Three times. So I answered. And it was Carys from the matching team.

> And she said there's a baby.

A *baby*. It's not meant to happen like that. A few weeks after panel. To be told there's a baby – Just born. Ready for us. If we want. I mean. It's not that simple.

A **flicker**. *Not quite a* **GLITCH**. **Mat** *almost doesn't acknowledge it.*

Carys says that it'd be an early permanence placement. Which we'd talked about. At the classes. And at panel – But we thought – We thought that we wouldn't end up doing that. That we'd go with someone a little bit older.

Because this way. This way you have to commit to the greyness of it. To the sort – of – but – sort – of – not – parenting – yet of it. Because with this, there's no guarantees yet. The birth family might get to have them back. That's what it's for.

It's to stop kids having to be the ones who are always moving around from placement to placement. This way they go to us. To foster them. So they know us, from the beginning. And they still get to see the birth family, but if that doesn't work out they just – stay. And we become mum and dad.

We understand it. Why it's a good thing. But we'd said to Sarah, we didn't know if we were cut out for it. The potential nothingness of it. The empty crib and the stars on the ceiling but no little person sitting in the middle. But now there was a baby. A boy.

And the matching lady – Carys – said that yes, this was *technically* a foster to adopt situation. But that she'd thought of us because it was already basically an open and shut case. He needed a family. His mum wasn't interested. We'd pick him up straight from the hospital. Can you imagine? We'd be there basically from day one. Day three. That's pretty much day one, isn't it?

How can you say no to that?

We went that weekend. To the NICU. And there he was. Little boy. LB.

Four pounds six ounces. I've never seen anything so small and so massive all at once. This perfect tiny little human. So we said yes. We started visiting. Every day. Only an hour or so at first. But then Mr Boggiani said I could start my adoption leave, so I'd go first thing in the morning and stay 'til the evening. Talking to him through the glass, so he could hear my voice. He looked like a little chicken. Under the lights, patches over his eyes. A perfect scrawny little chicken.

He had withdrawals. That's what the doctor said. His birth mum had been using loads of different stuff and his little body had got used to it too, to the constant stream of it into his blood. So when he'd come out. Early – Only a few weeks, not early, early. Even though he was tiny he wasn't early – early. But he had withdrawals. And that made him poorly. That and the jaundice and being so tiny. So I couldn't hold him. Not at the start. But I could stroke him. Through the little circles. I could stroke him and tell him my name and how excited we all were to be in his life now.

And when he was better, when the nurses took off the wires and the patches off his eyes and passed him to me, sat up in the chair. He was so titchy I thought he might fall straight through my fingers and break his tiny little head wide open on the floor.

But then he blinked right at me.

His eyes looked right into mine.

Saying 'hello you'. Like he knew all about me, already.

And there's no way he was going to let me let him fall.

So we sat there for a while. Looking at each other.

And then we took him home.

GLITCH

3

And it was bliss. It's been. Bliss.

I mean, there's been crying. There's been *lots* of crying. And he's had silent reflux and colic and cradle cap – Cradle cap that honestly made him look a little bit like his head was going to peel off. But he's been – perfect. For us. He's perfect for us. And we can't believe that this has happened. So soon. That – It's happening like this.

Because there's another couple – Paula and Sinead, we met them in the training and they're doing the early permanence thing too. They've got twins, they were placed with two nine-month-old little girls, which is amazing. They're gorgeous. We've had them round here. But their family. Not their dad. But their mum. Doesn't want them in care. She's trying her best, to get them back. So Paula and Sinead have to drive all the way to Stockport, two times a week, with the girls strapped in the back of the car. To go to a contact centre. So that their mum gets to see them.

Of course we'd do that – If that was something that was in LB's best interests. But we don't have to. Because his mum. His birth mum isn't interested at all. Or – That's not fair. It's not fair to say that she's not interested at all, I don't know that. But LB. She doesn't want contact. Left him at the hospital after he was born. Just – Got up and left. I mean, she checked he was alright. That he was in the NICU safe, someone from the social was coming. She'd told them, in advance that she didn't – She didn't want to keep him. That was the plan.

But then she just left. Before they could get all of the consents they needed. And there's no other family. So yeah, she's still on the scene, technically. But it's just a matter of paperwork. That's what everyone says.

Yeah, it's a Section 20. But it's not really.

He's ours. We're not supposed to call ourselves mum and dad. Not yet. But this is different to the normal set up. He's been with us since he was – Since forever in his little mind and it's not fair for him not to call *anyone* mum and dad. Is it? So when he starts babbling. We don't stop him. I'm not going to tell a baby who's saying "'Mmm-ma' not to do it, am I? I'm going to video him. And cry. And just. Feel like the luckiest human to have ever been a human.

Which is horrible. Really. When you think about it. To feel lucky. To feel like this was meant to happen. That he chose us – Because why should he have had to go through what he's been through? Why should his birth mum have to? If he was meant to happen why couldn't he just have been born to me or – I don't know. I tie myself up in knots. Thinking about it. Worrying about it. Worrying that something that started from such a sad and broken (and hopeless) place makes me feel like the luckiest person in the whole world. But it does. So I have to try to accept it. Being this – happy.

And I am happy. I'm so so so so happy. But the nights. The nights are dark. Because I want them to be light. For him to have so much light that he glows. And you have to work at that.

James has done this before. And he's a great dad. But Grace is eight now. So when he was doing this it was eight years ago. And even if it wasn't. Even if he'd only just done it. Grace is different to LB. And he hasn't read the things that I've read. About SIDS and bonding and (trauma) – I mean, he's done the training. We both did the training but he keeps telling me I'm doing amazing. Give myself a minute. Have a bath.

But I don't need a bath. I've had a shower. I've had a shower and I'm fine.

I just need to hold LB. I need to hold him and keep him safe and let him know that whenever he cries I'll be there. Everyone says they don't know how I do it. How I keep

going. But I do. Because I can't stop. I go and I go and I go.
We do baby groups and walks to the park – Even though he's
too little for the park – And we do the sensory things and the
routine. We have a really good routine. But sometimes he
cries so much he shakes. And it doesn't stop. It just keeps
coming.

The crying. And I'm desperate for it to stop. I'm desperate to
suck all of those feelings out of him and fill him up with
better ones. But I can't. He just sobs and shakes and I can't
cope. In that moment. That night. I didn't know how to
cope. How to make it better. And I couldn't put him down.
But nothing was working and I –

James   Let me try?

Mat *breathes again. Nods.*

She lies down.

*Another **flicker**. An almost **GLITCH**. It startles **Mat** straight back
up to standing.*

Carys is thrilled with us every time she sees us. She says she
knows that this is very unusual. This set up. But that we're
doing brilliantly. She's really proud of us. It won't be much
longer. We won't have to wait much longer for the paperwork
to be sorted, for us to go to court. We just have to be patient.
And we can do that.

Of course we can do that. Because this is all going to work
out in the end.

What's for you won't go past you. That's what my Gareth
says. And I can't imagine now – I can't imagine a world
where LB goes past me.

He's doing so well now. And yeah, he's not meeting all of his
milestones yet. But he's getting there. And Grace adores
him. She can't get enough of his little laugh. He's nothing
like the scrawny little bird he was when he was born
anymore. He's massive. Loves his bottles and the finger

foods he's allowed now. He loves chomping down on something tasty. He's always eating. Not in an unhealthy way. Just in a gorgeous way. He's gorgeous. He's getting bigger and bigger and smilier and smilier and when Grace is at home she just carries him everywhere. On her hip, like a little mum. He's half her size but she never puts him down.

And when people stop us in the street. When Grace is home and we go to the park or to the tesco's or when we go to the coffee shop, next to her ballet class. People always laugh and say how much Grace looks like her dad. Because they do. They've always looked like little and large. They're carbon copies of each other. People have always said it. But *now*. Now people say that she's her dad's twin, but that the little boy – They say his smile is just like mine.

And it is.

I know it's not – actually – But he does. Look like me. The way he takes in the world.

We weren't wearing superhero costumes when the next call came.

We were stood at a fish counter. In the Morrisons in St Helens. The one round the corner from Gareth's. He's been under the weather for the last few weeks, so we said we'd call in. James said he'd make us all dinner, so we'd walked to Morrisons to get the bits. LB in his little red pram, Grace hiding behind it because she was freaked out by the eyeballs on the fish. I didn't like the look of an octopus that was definitely on the turn – Nobody in St Helens is going to buy an octopus – Whoever put that order in had clearly fucked up that day. James was trying to convince me to let him buy it. Saying he'd be able to do something delicious with it. Turn it into tempura or something and I was saying that he'd be better off just getting the fish pie mix that we know Gareth likes when Carys rang.

Carys the social worker.

We hadn't spoken for a while. She was still chasing up the final paper work, said she's be in touch as soon as it was done. So I thought that that was what she was ringing to say. LB was grizzling in his pram, because he was hot. He gets hot really easily, so I lifted him out, had him on my hip with one hand and the phone in my other, but it was still synced up with my headphones. So I couldn't hear Carys properly. I had to pass LB to James and he didn't like that, he wanted a cwtch. That's what James was saying, he wanted a cwtch with his mum so I told Carys to hold on for a second. Sorted the phone out. Said hello all excited. Thought this was going to be the moment. The life changing moment. The good news.

But it wasn't.

Or it was. It was good news for somebody. Just. Not us.

It was good news for LB. Because his grandma. His real grandma. His birth mum's mum. Had gotten in touch.

Her name was Jackie. And she wanted him back.

GLITCH: *Everything feels slow. Like **Mat**'s moving through treacle. And then suddenly it's fast. Too fast.*

4

James didn't want me to go. He didn't want us to have anything to do with – her. He says

James   Little boy is our little boy. We're his mum and dad. She can't just. Waltz in and – take that away from him.

But we're not. We're not actually his mum and dad. Are we. He calls us that. I told you, he calls us that. And even Carys knows he does. We told her and she just – gave us a wink and said that we don't need to worry. This was a done deal.

Paula and Sinead. Paula and Sinead and the twins. They went to court. Last week. They went to court last week, and the court decided – They said that they should be the parents. And that's what they're going to be. But those girls. Those girls call their birth mum mum. Because they've seen her. Two times a week, every week. And they're going to carry on – having contact. It won't be as much, but they're going to carry on having contact. And Paula and Sinead are going to be their mums. Nobody thought that was going to happen. Nobody thought that was going to happen but they all – They all thought that LB was going to be our LB forever. It was a done deal. That's what Carys said.

And now – Now it isn't. All of a sudden. It's just. Not. Not a deal. No deal. Like Noel Edmunds has been sitting in my nightmares, making sure they come true.

And we have to take LB to meet Jackie. That's what Carys says. We have to facilitate it.

> She knows that that's a lot to ask though – in the circumstances . . .

In the circumstances, that's what she said, like it was just a little cock up with the paperwork and not the idea that our baby suddenly might not be our baby any more. She said that we didn't have to physically take him. If that would be too tough. She was happy to take him to the contact centre herself. Sending him with a stranger to meet a stranger.

James said that's what we should do, that we shouldn't make it easy for them –

But how was I supposed to let that happen? This isn't. What we wanted – What we planned. But it was – part of the deal – hypothetically. Hypothetically we knew that we had to do this, if we were agreeing to early permanence. But I don't want to say that to James. Because he's hurting. That's why he's hurting so much, because he knows that this is what we have to do.

And he can't face it. He can't do it himself. But I can. So we take the bus.

I could have driven. James says I should have driven. Or asked Gareth to help, but –

But if we'd driven, I'd have had to strap him into the car seat.

And I don't want that. Not now. I want to feel his skin next to my skin. I don't want to let him go. Not unless I absolutely have to. I want to keep him as close to me as possible.

And normally he's a wriggler. He wriggles everywhere, can't sit still. But on that bus ride – It was sort of like he knew what I – what we needed. To be close. Heart by heart. And he curled into me like he used to do when he was tiny. All soft and heavy and there. And I held him so tightly that I thought I might scream.

I wanted to hate her.

I wanted to really, really hate her.

I wanted her to be a horrible, horrible person who had nothing to give LB. Some chancer who'd just showed up because she thought there might be something in it for her. Someone the court would see straight through.

But we walked into the contact centre. The one in town. And it was quiet and empty and I thought we'd got there first.

But then I saw her.

And she reminded me of my nNan.

My little nan who'd always been there. When my mum was being difficult. When it wasn't safe to sleep at home. Who'd walked through the rain to make sure I had an umbrella and a proper pair of shoes on the way home from school when it was pissing it down outside. Who made me feel safe and held and like I was someone that somebody loved.

And I wanted to cry.

I wanted to turn straight back around, grab LB and sob while we ran as fast as we could in the other direction.

But I saw Jackie – And she looked at LB the way my nan used to look at me.

And I knew. I just knew. That she hadn't known before now. There was no world in which this woman could have known that this little boy had existed before now. Because she'd have been there. From the first day. She'd have been in the hospital with the wires and the doctors and the worries. She wouldn't have missed a second.

And I was right. Because as they were playing – She was really good at playing with him. He went straight to her – She told me that she hadn't known. Her daughter hadn't told her.

Jackie hardly saw her. Her daughter. Not because she didn't want to – But because she couldn't. It wasn't safe. For the other children. Little boy has a brother and a sister.

And my heart felt like it was – I don't have the words for how my heart felt when I heard that. Because he has a brother and a sister. Who are just like him. Which is – amazing – But all I could see was Grace smiling with him on her hip.

They were a long way from here. The brother and the sister. In Jackie's house. But they were there. And they were waiting.

And I felt like I was falling. Like the world was moving too fast and too slow and too everything all at the same time. But no matter what happened. No matter how I tried to make the world make sense again in my head, Jackie was there. And she was his nan. And he smiled when he saw her too.

It didn't take a long time. It took just under a year to get to where we were. Before the phone call. To the family we'd become. Our little four.

But it took less than six weeks for him to be gone. To the other side of the country.

Jackie says I can see him, when he's settled.

Maybe a few times a year. Not too many.

Can you imagine that? To go from. From every day. Every minute. Breathing him in – Hearing his laugh and holding him to – A few times a year?

Because I can't. My brain can't imagine that world yet. It can't wrap itself around that possibility. That reality. I wake in the night and feel like I'm going to die. That's what this feels like. Like I'm dying.

I wanted to go with him. To Hull. I wanted to get him comfortable. Do it in stages. That made the most sense – To me.

But Jackie said it would unsettle the other children.

And she gets to make the decisions. Not me. Not us.

We don't get to decide anything now. We're just – facilitators. That's what we have to do. The court decided that LB should be with his family – With his birth family. They said. They said at the hearing, how appreciative they were. Of everything we'd done. Of how difficult a situation it was. But that it was in his best interests to be with his birth family.

And logically, I know that that makes sense. My brain knows that. But I can't. I can't turn off the rest of my body.

I wanted to send him with all of his things. His clothes and his shoes and his teddies and his trains and the soft play bits – The soft play bits we'd got him for Christmas that he loves jumping on in the living room – And then I thought maybe we should send the bed too? We'd made it – Gareth and James had made it – because he'd been pulling himself up on the bars of the crib. And he's still not even one but he'd managed to hook his leg over it, so Gareth and James had turned it into a bed. A proper little bed and he loves it. He loves his big boy bed so I said to Jackie that we could hire a van – Drive it over. But she said that there wouldn't be enough space. She doesn't need to have a spare room. If you're a kinship carer – A special guardian. They don't make you have a spare room, so – So, little boy and his brother and sister were going to share. They're all going to share a room together. And that will be great. I know he'll love that, but now I wish that I'd let Grace sleep in his room every time she'd asked. Even when I knew that it'd stop him from falling asleep. I wish we'd all just piled in there every night. Made the floor a massive bed, mattresses from wall to wall. A nest. I wish we'd made it a nest for all of us to bury down into together.

But it's too late. He's going. And Jackie says that I should just put a few of his favourite few bits in a bag – Not a suitcase, there was no point, she'd unpack them as soon as they got there. She told me I didn't need to worry. She'd make sure he was comfy.

And I know she will.

It was meant to be Jackie, collecting him. She was meant to be meeting us, at the contact centre. That's what we'd arranged. But this morning. This morning I got the phone call and it was Carys and she said that little boy's sister was poorly, so she couldn't come. And for a second I thought that meant we'd have more time. Another night.

That's all I want, another night. Because last night was lovely. It was beautiful – We did the best that we could. We spent the whole day at the park. On that tea cup. The spinning tea cup that he loves but that makes me and James feel sick. We both just took it in turns. Spinning us round again and again and again until we couldn't even feel our faces we were so cold. And it bucketed down and Grace and Gareth had baked a cake. A massive cake with Mr Duck on. Because LB loves Mr Duck. And we had a picky tea, on a bath towel in the living room. And we played on the soft play and LB looked like he couldn't believe his luck – Having us all together in the same space. And we told him we loved him. We all told him how much we loved him even though he doesn't really know what we're saying. And we showed him the photo book we'd made. With all our pictures. But it says Mat and James now. Underneath. Not (Mum and Dad).

And it was. It was perfect. But we could do it again tonight. We could do it again for a week, if Jackie had to look after his little sister – It was no bother at all, we don't mind doing that –

But Carys says that's not going to happen. We need to bring him to the contact centre today. And then a social worker will drive him to Hull.

We were all going to go together – To see him off. But Grace was too upset. She couldn't do it. So James stayed behind with her. He gave LB the biggest hug. Blew a massive raspberry on his belly. And that was that.

Gareth drove. We sang songs in the car. Happy Birthday mostly. It's not his birthday but he loves that song. Loves anyone's birthday. The candles. So we just kept singing it. Pretending to blow them out. Gareth was great.

But I walked him in by myself. I wanted to do that.

To be the last person to kiss his little legs before they were bundled into a car.

And I was. I told him I loved him. And then I said goodbye. And I didn't cry. I didn't come back when he called me. When he said Mum. I left.

Mat *walks back into NOW. Her story is back where it started.*

NOW

*Total silence. **Mat** takes in where she is. Starts to take it apart. Then she catches hold of the smell of LB. Can't let go. Lies in the middle of it. Frozen.*

*There's a knock at the door. There are lots of soft knocks at the door. But **Mat** can't move. We hear **James** trying to get through to her. Softly. Then not so softly. Then softly again. Even though she doesn't reply. He keeps trying. Days pass as we hear variations on:*

James Mat?   **James** I've got you a cup of tea.

          James Please Mat –   **James** Babe, open the –

          James Mat I need to –

               James Please let me in Mat.

                    James Mat?

*A new day. **Mat**'s still there. There's a knock.*

James You don't need to come out.
              But Grace has something to tell you –

Grace We've done the big clean!

The room fills with light.

SOON

Sometimes I sit outside. When Grace is at school.

And I play videos of him. Of little boy, in the park. On the teacup. Or on the swing.

And I play them loudly and I close my eyes and I pretend he's there still.

It's been six months. Almost.

And we were talking last night about – Everything. Without really talking about it. Which we do a lot. But then James said out of nowhere that he doesn't think he could do it again. Go through (everything) – again.

And I know it's too early. It's too early yet to talk about the future. He's in pain. (We both are.)

So I didn't say it to James. But this pain. This pain shouldn't be in a kid should it? This feeling of *loss*. Kids shouldn't have to feel this. This is what I felt. When I was little. But LB. We've protected LB from that feeling because this way – This way he's gone straight from us to Jackie and his brother and sister and he's safe and loved from all angles – And when he's grown up. When he's grown up, he's going to have everything we've sent him. To look back on. Or to visit – If that's what he wants –

And I don't want to say it yet.

So I won't.

Because it's too soon. I know that.

And because I know that me thinking about it – or saying it – will make some people think that. That what we've been through, what we're feeling now. Isn't really grief. They'll think that little boy means less to me than he does. But that's wrong. Because he's everything.

But if we did (decide to) – And if this – happened. Again. Then we could survive it. Because we've survived this. We're surviving this. And this is a good thing.

Us. And what we're doing. What we've done.

This is a good thing.

END

ACKNOWLEDGEMENTS

Thank you to Lucy Fawcett for being the greatest agent and person. I am so very lucky to have you. Thanks too to Rebecca Lyon and David Taylor for everything you have ever done for me. Thanks to Sian Carter and all at Methuen for bringing Mat's journey to print.

Attachment was originally developed for television with Warp Films. Thank you to Mark Herbert, Cicely Hadman, Robin Gutch and Kasheina Vencatasawmy for believing in me back in 2019. It is thanks to Toby Parsons Productions that I was able to adapt that original television script into a one woman show for stage. Thank you to Toby for his commitment to developing new writing for theatre in a time when so few producers feel able to take risks. Thanks to Julia Samuels for her insight, direction and kindness and to Patricia Verity Suarez who helped me to think about Mat's physical language during our early stages of research and development.

Thank you to Lindsay Rodden and Suzanne Bell for accepting eighteen-year-old me onto the Everyman's Young Writers Programme when I was feeling lost. And to Frank Peschier for bringing me back into the building all these years later. Thanks to Nathan Powell for being such a wonderful creative director and for your faith in this play. Thanks to Tommo Fowler for being brilliant and quite possibly the most supportive dramaturgical brain of all time. Sam Longville you are a delight and I am so pleased to have you as *Attachment*'s producer. Thanks also to Ashlie Nelson for being the first person to react to Grace's voice in exactly the way I hoped.

Thank you to Sam Freeman, Laurie Coldwell, Helena Seneca, Niall Wilson, Rebecca Crookshank, Jack Hudson, Helen Simmons and Max Toomey who have each answered panicked late-night requests for notes with love. Thanks also to Stefanie Zuber for answering every question I had with such grace and insight.

Noel Jones, Kieran Sing and Ellie Light you are gorgeous creatives and I am so lucky to work with you. Elliott Kingsley and Debbie Brannan, your generosity, kindness and talent was indispensable to this production. Paislie Reid you are everything I ever dreamt that Mat could be and so much more. Kate Treadell I've been obsessed with you for the longest time and will be forever.

Thank you to my parents for taking me to the theatre. To Jan for holding our family together and to Nin for bursting my heart wide open.

Most importantly, thank you to every person who has spoken to me over the years about their journeys through the UK's care system. Your stories have shaped so much of what *Attachment* is, I hope that we've done you proud.